FATHER
GROPPI

Other Badger Biographies

FATHER GROPPI

Marching for Civil Rights

STUART STOTTS

WISCONSIN HISTORICAL SOCIETY PRESS

Published by the Wisconsin Historical Society Press
Publishers since 1855

©2013 by the State Historical Society of Wisconsin

wisconsin history.org

Photographs identified with WHi are from the Society's collections; address requests to reproduce these photos to the Visual Materials Archivist at the Wisconsin Historical Society, 816 State Street, Madison, WI 53706.

Printed in Wisconsin, U.S.A.
Designed by Jill Bremigan

17 16 15 14 13   1 2 3 4 5

Library of Congress Cataloging-in-Publication Data
Stotts, Stuart, 1957-
  Father Groppi : marching for civil rights / Stuart Stotts. — 1st edition.
    pages cm. — (Badger biographies)
  Includes bibliographical references and index.
  ISBN 978-0-87020-575-0 (paperback : alkaline paper) 1. Groppi, James, 1930-1985—Juvenile literature. 2. Civil rights workers—United States—Biography—Juvenile literature. 3. Civil rights workers—Wisconsin—Milwaukee—Biography—Juvenile literature. 4. Priests—Wisconsin—Milwaukee—Biography—Juvenile literature. 5. Catholic Church—Wisconsin—Milwaukee—Clergy—Biography—Juvenile literature. 6. African Americans—Civil rights—History—20th century—Juvenile literature. 7. African Americans—Civil rights—Wisconsin—Milwaukee—History—20th century—Juvenile literature. 8. Civil rights movements—United States—History—20th century—Juvenile literature. 9. Civil rights movements—Wisconsin—Milwaukee—History—20th century—Juvenile literature. 10. Milwaukee (Wis.)—Race relations—History—20th century—Juvenile literature. I. Title.
  E185.98.G76S76 2013
  323.092—dc23
  [B]
                         2012029610

∞ The paper used in this publication meets the minimum requirements of the American National Standard for Information Sciences—Permanence of Paper for Printed Library Materials, ANSI Z39.48-1992.

This book is dedicated to Laurie Ellen Neustadt (1954-1999),
a tireless fighter for peace, justice, and equality,
and my dear friend.

Publication of this book was made possible in part by a grant
from the D.C. Everest fellowship fund.

Contents

1

Meet Father Groppi

Father James Groppi was a leader in the **civil rights movement** in Wisconsin. In the late 1960s, he worked with thousands of people in Milwaukee as they **demanded** good houses, better schools, and equal rights for African Americans.

Father Groppi was not a rich man or an elected official. He was raised in a hardworking family and had an average education. But he cared deeply about equality. Even though he was white, he spoke out for black people's rights.

The civil rights movement was about changing laws and opinions. It was about good jobs, safe neighborhoods, and respect for African Americans. It was about people from all over the country, black and white, working together to improve the lives of African Americans.

civil rights movement: the movement during the mid-1950s and 1960s for African Americans to be treated fairly and equally under the law   **demanded**: officially and strongly requested

The story of the civil rights movement begins far from Wisconsin and long before Father Groppi's time. **Discrimination** and **racism** have a long history in the United States.

Racism and Discrimination

What are racism and discrimination? Racism is the belief that one race is better than another. In the United States, white people have often thought they are better than black people. White racists made laws that limited the freedom of black people, or they bullied or **threatened** them.

These actions were discrimination. Discrimination is when people are treated unequally through laws, **customs**, or behaviors. Racism is about how people think, and discrimination is about how they act.

The civil rights movement fought these problems, but racism and discrimination are still with us today.

Racism and discrimination against black people in the United States began with slavery. In the late 1500s, black people were bought or captured in Africa and brought to

discrimination: unfair treatment of people, based on differences such as race, age, or place of birth
racism: the belief that one race is better than another   **threatened**: told someone they will be hurt if they don't do as they are told   **custom**: a habit or common practice of a group of people

2

America to work on **plantations** in the South. Racist people believed Africans weren't equal to white people and could be bought and sold as slaves.

Slaves didn't have the same rights as other people. They were forced to work very hard, and they were often treated poorly. They were beaten if they didn't do what they were told, and children could be sold away from their parents. Some Americans thought slavery was wrong, and disagreement about slavery divided the country, leading to the Civil War in 1861.

Slaves were freed after the war, but black people throughout the country still faced discrimination. Many of them couldn't vote, couldn't eat in some restaurants, and couldn't live in certain parts of town, just because of their skin color.

Black people fought for their rights, but change came slowly.

plantation: a large farm

LIBRARY OF CONGRESS, PRINTS & PHOTOGRAPHS DIVISION, FSA/OWI COLLECTION, LC-USF33-030700-M1

Discrimination and segregation were common in the South. Only white people were allowed to go through this door to the Farmers Cafe in Durham, North Carolina.

LIBRARY OF CONGRESS, PRINTS & PHOTOGRAPHS DIVISION, FSA/OWI COLLECTION, LC-DIG-PPMSC-00201

At this bus station in Tennessee, black people were not allowed in the white waiting room.

In the 1950s, the struggle for equality sped up. People who believed racism was wrong worked together to **protest** unfair laws and discrimination. Sometimes protesters helped change the way people thought, but often they were attacked, threatened, or thrown in jail. Together these protests were known as the civil rights movement, and they became a powerful force for change.

When most people think about the civil rights movement, they think of the southern United States. It was in the South that discrimination against black people was strongest. In the South, the famous people of the movement, like Rosa Parks and Martin Luther King Jr., led the battle for equal rights. And there, in the South, thousands of other people who weren't famous at all changed history by protesting the unfair ways black people were treated.

Almost all of the well-known events of the civil rights movement happened in the South. But black people faced **inequality** throughout the United States.

protest: gather and speak out in public to fight for a cause   **inequality**: unfair differences between people

The struggle for equality involved many issues. What were these protesters demanding?

In the 1960s, the civil rights movement arrived in the North. Black people in cities like Milwaukee began to demand equal rights. People came together to protest inequality. They faced violence and were arrested, just as civil rights workers in the South were.

The civil rights movement in the North had leaders too. Father James Groppi was one of them. He was born in

Milwaukee and grew up in a neighborhood where no black people lived. In fact, when he was young, he hardly ever saw black people because Milwaukee was **segregated**. Black people lived in a different part of town, away from where James grew up.

Even though James Groppi didn't understand much about civil rights when he was a kid, by the time he was a young man, he had learned a lot. As the son of an Italian **immigrant**, James experienced discrimination himself. He knew how it felt to be called names and laughed at just because of who you are and where you came from.

When James grew up, he became a Catholic priest. He often worked for churches in poor neighborhoods, and he saw how black people suffered. As he became aware of the **injustice** black people faced, Father Groppi decided he had to do something. He organized protests and led the fair housing **marches**, Wisconsin's best-known civil rights event. He was willing to stand up for what he believed, even if it meant facing violence or going to jail.

segregated: separated for the purpose of keeping groups apart based on the color of their skin
immigrant (**im** uh gruhnt): someone who leaves a country to permanently live in another country
injustice: unfairness or lack of justice   **march**: a protest where a lot of people join together publicly to express their opinion about something by walking from one place to another

7

Father Groppi helped to bring the civil rights movement north. In his time, he became famous around the country. But he didn't think he was doing something special. He just knew he couldn't stand by when he saw discrimination. He had to speak up and work with others for a more equal and just society.

What makes a person want to stand up for someone else? Why would a white man like Father Groppi face violence, **threats**, and insults so that black people would be treated better? And how does this priest from Milwaukee fit into the bigger history of the civil rights movement?

This is the story of Father Groppi and the fight for equal rights in Wisconsin.

threat: a warning that harm will come if something is not done

2

Early Years

James Groppi began to understand discrimination when he was just a kid growing up on the south side of Milwaukee.

James was born on November 16, 1930. His father, **Giocondo**, was an Italian immigrant. When Giocondo first came to the United States, he sold balloons and soap door to door. Later he opened a small grocery store in the Bay View neighborhood of Milwaukee.

James's mother, **Giorgina**, also came from an Italian family. Both of James's parents had moved to America from a town called **Lucca** near Rome, Italy. James was the second youngest of 12 children, but 2 of his **siblings** died before he was born. James worked alongside his older brothers and sisters in the family grocery store.

Giocondo: juh **kawn** doh   **Giorgina**: jawr **jee** nuh   **Lucca**: **loo** kuh   **sibling** (**sib** ling): a brother or sister

WHI IMAGE ID 52837

Downtown Milwaukee in 1930

When James was growing up, the south side of Milwaukee was for whites and the north side was for African Americans. James lived in Bay View on the south side, and families there were mostly from Ireland and Poland. They lived in small, tidy houses and worked in local factories. Most people were Catholic, and many children went to Catholic schools instead of public ones.

Milwaukee Neighborhoods

The **Menomonee** River divides Milwaukee into the north and south sides. Long bridges, called **viaducts**, reach across the river valley to connect the 2 sides. Milwaukee has neighborhoods on both sides of the river.

In James's day, families who came from the same **ethnic** background or from the same country, like Ireland, Poland, or Germany, usually lived near each other in their own neighborhood. The boundaries between neighborhoods

The Menomonee River is in a shallow valley. Viaducts like this one for Grand Avenue span the whole valley, passing over houses and businesses that sit below.

weren't always obvious, but everyone knew where they were. If you came from one neighborhood, it could be dangerous or at least uncomfortable to go into a different one. People didn't like outsiders.

Menomonee: muh **nah** muh nee   **viaduct** (**vi** uh duhkt): a large bridge that often crosses a valley or city street   **ethnic:** having to do with a group of people sharing the same home country or culture

11

Bay View residents were trying to build a better life for themselves. Although they worked hard, spent time with friends and family, and mostly lived quiet lives, the neighborhood had a history of standing up for people's rights.

Forty-five years before James was born, thousands of workers protested the number of hours they had to work at the Bay View Rolling Mills factory. At the time, it was common to work 10, 12, or even 14 hours a day. Many workers thought that was too much. They believed that they should only have to work 8 hours a day, as most people do now.

On May 5, 1886, about 1,500 people marched in the Bay View neighborhood to demand a shorter workday. The governor of Wisconsin, Jeremiah Rusk, called in the **National Guard** because he was afraid the marchers would become violent. When the crowd approached a factory, members of the National Guard became nervous and fired their guns at them. Seven people died in what became known as the Bay View **Massacre**. Although the marchers were not successful at the time, workers throughout the country were eventually granted the right to have a shorter workday.

National Guard: a volunteer military that is commanded by each state's governor
massacre (**mass** uh ker): a cruel act of killing innocent or defenseless people

The massacre happened before the Groppis came to Milwaukee, but Bay View residents remembered the protests and the massacre. To them it was a powerful example of ordinary people standing up for their rights. The neighborhood story reminded James and others about how people can come together to try to make their lives better.

WHI IMAGE ID 7015

The Bay View Rolling Mills built metal objects.

Like many other children in his neighborhood, James attended **Immaculate Conception**, a Catholic elementary and middle school. The nuns who taught him were tough on students. They had lots of rules and punished students firmly. Later, James went to Bay View High School, which was a public school. He said that after his **strict** Catholic school, he had a "four-year vacation in high school."

Immaculate Conception: i **mak** yuh lit kuhn **sep** shun   **strict**: making someone follow all the rules

WHI IMAGE ID 92290

James as a young man holding a basketball.

James was tall, with dark hair. He described himself as a little wild when he was young. "We used to do **juvenile** things," he said, "like throw firecrackers in the barroom **spittoons**."

juvenile (**joo** vuh nuhl): childish and immature   **spittoon** (spi **toon**): a small bucket that people spit into when they are chewing tobacco

He was a good athlete, and he loved basketball. He showed that he could be a leader. In his last 2 years at Bay View High School, he started at **guard**, and he was captain of the team in his senior year.

Some early experiences with discrimination helped shape the ideas that James would later live by. He first learned about **tolerance** in his family.

When James's father arrived in Milwaukee in 1913, large numbers of Italians were just beginning to come to the United States. They were discriminated against by other ethnic groups in Milwaukee and were made fun of for their customs. Giocondo Groppi thought this was wrong, so he didn't allow his children to show **prejudice** toward others. He wouldn't permit them to say words that put anyone down. James was raised in a family that taught tolerance and respect, even though many of his neighbors were open about their prejudices.

In the 1930s, when James was young, Italians in Milwaukee still experienced discrimination. His family's church,

guard: a basketball player who runs the plays on the team   **tolerance**: the willingness to accept the customs or beliefs of other people   **prejudice** (**prej** uh dis): treatment of others based on unfair judgment of them

Immaculate Conception, was mostly an Irish church, and James later said that his family never felt welcome there because they weren't Irish. He recalled that an Italian priest would lead a separate **Mass** for Italians at a shoemaker's shop in the neighborhood. He also remembered sitting in class at Bay View High one day when an Italian American made announcements over the loudspeaker. Everyone made fun of his **accent**, and James felt embarrassed.

James had little contact with black people. However, during a basketball game between Bay View and Milwaukee's Lincoln High School, James blocked a driving player, who happened to be black, and knocked him down. When James offered to help him up, the player kicked James in the stomach. Both players later apologized to each other.

In school, James wrote about that experience in an **essay** discussing **brotherhood** and race. He believed it was an example of people from different backgrounds showing respect to each other and solving a problem. It was an idea that became important later in James's life.

Mass: the main religious service in the Catholic Church **accent** (**ak** sent): the way you pronounce words and put them together **essay**: a piece of writing about a particular subject **brotherhood**: warm and good feelings toward all people, as if they were the same as your own brothers or sisters

When James graduated from high school, he wasn't sure what he wanted to do. He didn't have a direction for his life. He worked setting up pins in a bowling alley, and he played basketball with friends. A year later, he enrolled at Mount Calvary **Seminary** in Fond du Lac, Wisconsin, where he studied from 1950 to 1952. He later attended St. Francis Seminary near Milwaukee and graduated in 1959.

When asked why he studied at a seminary, James replied, "I didn't see anything around. To

PHOTOGRAPH COURTESY OF THE MILWAUKEE JOURNAL SENTINEL

St. Francis Seminary

seminary: a school that trains students to become priests, ministers, or rabbis

me, life, in order to have meaning, had to have religion. . . . You're here today and you're gone the next day. You've got to do something in this short expanse of time to make **eternity** meaningful."

James saw his life as more than just getting a job and raising a family. He wanted to improve the lives of many people and make a difference in the world, and he thought becoming a priest would help him do that.

eternity: all of time, from the beginning to the end

3

Entering the Priesthood

In between his time studying at the seminaries, James had a job driving a city bus. In 1956, he also began to work at **Blessed** Martin's Youth Center in Milwaukee. The youth center offered activities and help for neighborhood children. Many of the kids who hung out there were African American. One of them called James "Mr. Droopy Pants" because he always wore big, baggy pants. Despite James's appearance, children at the center loved him.

A Milwaukee city bus like the one James drove

blessed: bles id

James took the children to parks during the day, playing games and making lunches. On weekends he took older kids on camping trips and to baseball and basketball games. James had fun with the children, but he also learned about their lives. "Black people were teaching me, even when they were not aware of it," he said. "They were erasing from my mind **stereotypes** that every white person thought."

Children from Blessed Martin's Youth Center putting on a Christmas pageant

stereotype: an overly simple idea or opinion of a person, group, or thing

Prejudice and Stereotypes

Prejudice, like racism, is the belief that a group of people is **inferior** to another. One person judges another person before getting to know that person, based on his or her skin color or background.

Prejudice is based on stereotypes, where a person believes that everyone from a group is the same. For example, someone might have a stereotype of black people as poor or lazy, and as a result think badly of every black person he or she meets.

When someone looks at another person in this way, they can't see who that person really is—all they see is what they already think. It becomes easy to discriminate against a group because prejudice and stereotypes make people think everyone from that group can be treated the same.

James remembered one troubling event. One of the black girls at the youth center was named Loretta. "She usually got along with everyone and was constantly looking out for others," James recalled.

One day a white kid walked past her and called her a racist name. "It hurt her really bad. She was crushed," said James.

inferior (in **feer** ee ur): not as good

"After a young person has been hurt a number of times like that, you begin to react." James saw firsthand the prejudice and suffering that black people experienced as part of their daily lives.

The Words We Use

We refer to people of a different color or race in many ways. In James's time, black people were often called "colored" or "negro." These terms are rarely used today. It's more acceptable now to use "black" or "African American" when speaking of people of that race.

There are also many words that people use for African Americans that are unacceptable and insulting, and which show the prejudice or racism of the person using them. As people confront racism, they often examine and change the words they use, to eliminate offensive or hurtful terms. By changing the words we use, we begin to change the ideas that lie behind them.

James found that prejudice existed in the seminary as well, and he was shocked by some of the other students' actions and words. He was upset when his class put on a **minstrel**

minstrel (**min** struhl): a performer who sings songs, tells stories and jokes, and recites poetry

show. Minstrel shows were a popular form of entertainment in the nineteenth century. White people wore black makeup to make themselves look like African Americans. They sang, danced, and told jokes, but they also made black people look stupid, lazy, and **superstitious**. Minstrel shows were popular until around 1900, but **amateurs** continued to put them on after that, often to make fun of black people.

WHI IMAGE ID 63833

A group of white people dressed up to put on a minstrel show

James refused to attend. "They could not see that this was insulting to the black community," he said. "They could not see that here again the negro was being **portrayed** as a poor, meek, **docile**, musical creature."

superstitious: believing things that are based on fear or hope, and not on facts   amateur (am uh chur): someone who performs without getting paid for it   portrayed: shown in a certain way   docile (dahs uhl): calm and easy to lead or teach

After he graduated from seminary in 1959, James was **ordained** into the priesthood. He was assigned to St. Veronica, a white **parish** church on Milwaukee's south side, where he worked for 4 years. As a priest, he performed weddings and funerals. He comforted people when they were sick or sad. He taught about the Bible and church beliefs.

Gradually, Father Groppi's interest in helping others expanded

WHI IMAGE ID 92287

Father Groppi loved being a priest. He believed it gave meaning to his life.

ordained: officially made a priest or minister   **parish**: the area and people that a single church is responsible for

beyond his **congregation** and his neighborhood. He knew
that the members of his church had many prejudices against
other races and ethnic groups. He wanted to change these
prejudices because the Bible says that people should love
everyone, not just those from a similar background.

After attending a community meeting about discrimination
in housing, Father Groppi preached for 10 Sundays in a row
on racial justice. "I wanted to let them know where I stood,"
he said. He also wanted to change the way the members of
his parish thought and acted.

A few years later, when Father Groppi challenged
Milwaukee's housing laws, he marched and protested on the
south side, near his old parish. Although some of his past
parish members supported him, others met him with insults
and threats. The prejudice there was still strong.

In 1963, church leaders moved Father Groppi from
St. Veronica to St. **Boniface**, a north-side parish that was almost
all black. The church members at St. Boniface came to love
Father Groppi. Children and adults respected and **admired**

congregation: the group of people who come together for a church service   **Boniface: bah** nuh fis
admired: liked and looked up to

25

him. They knew he cared deeply about them. He listened to their stories and did what he could to help. He also loved to have fun with the children.

One member of the church later said, "He was always surrounded by children, each one tugging at or hugging some small part of him, wanting to be close to this man they all loved. ... There in a corner sat Father Jim Groppi, surrounded by a **gaggle** of children. A toddler just beginning to walk seated on his lap, five-year-olds tugging at his pants leg, nine-year-olds hanging over his shoulders as he tried to talk."

The more Father Groppi saw the lives of his **inner-city** congregation, the more he understood injustice. He said later, "When I came to St. Boniface, the suffering I saw! Here I was and all I had to give people was that I was a priest. But the woman across the street wanted to know what to do about her **slum landlord** who was charging a huge amount and wouldn't fix up anything. The young people wanted to know what they should do about getting a job, and young couples were getting married who wanted to get **decent** housing."

gaggle: a group   **inner-city**: having to do with the downtown or central part of a city, usually the poorer and most populated parts of it   **slum landlord**: someone who owns a building for rent but doesn't take good care of it   **decent** (**dee** suhnt): acceptable or satisfactory

St. Boniface Church

Father Groppi wanted to help. But he was also torn. Part of him wanted to be a respectable priest: take care of church families, **baptize** babies, visit the sick, and preach sermons. But there were many in the Catholic Church who felt that priests should not talk about **political** issues like prejudice and discrimination. In the end, he decided to become more

baptize (bap tiz): to sprinkle water on someone's head or dunk him or her in water as a sign that the person has become a Christian   **political** (puh **lit** uh kuhl): having to do with the way a city, state, or nation governs itself

involved in civil rights. His conscience and love for his church members wouldn't allow him to be silent in the face of injustice.

Father Groppi's time at St. Boniface shaped his understanding of civil rights. He learned even more as he became involved in the national civil rights movement.

4

The National Civil Rights Movement

Father Groppi knew the history of slavery in the United States. He knew about the Civil War and how slaves were freed. In his work as a priest, he had also learned that even though African Americans were free, discrimination and prejudice continued. They did not have the same rights as others, especially in the South, where slavery had been **legal**. Discrimination was particularly strong there, and many laws supported it.

Keeping black and white people apart by law is called segregation, and segregation was everywhere in the South. On buses, black people could not sit in the same sections as white people. In schools and other public buildings, they could not drink from the same water fountains. Often, they could not vote or hold certain jobs or go to good schools. They were not allowed to eat in the same restaurants as

legal: allowed by law

29

white people or get treated in the same hospitals. It was even against the law for a white person to marry a black person.

LIBRARY OF CONGRESS, PRINTS & PHOTOGRAPHS DIVISION, FSA/OWI COLLECTION, LC-DIG-FSA-8A032282

In the South, it was common for white and black people to have separate drinking fountains, like this one for "colored" people in North Carolina.

In the 1950s and 1960s, black people challenged racism, discrimination, and segregation in the South. In 1955, Rosa Parks sparked a bus **boycott** in Montgomery, Alabama, when she refused to give up her seat on the bus to a white person. In 1957, in Little Rock, Arkansas, 9 African American teenagers **integrated** Central High School, although they needed the US Army to protect them. In 1960, black students in Greensboro,

boycott: refusing to buy something or use a service as a protest   **integrated**: made to include people of all races

North Carolina, held **sit-ins** at a lunch counter, demanding that black people be allowed to eat with white people. In 1961, black and white "freedom riders" rode buses together through the South, calling for an end to segregation in transportation.

The civil rights movement was growing. Thousands of people joined marches and **rallies**. They **registered** to vote. They integrated restaurants and other public places. Some protesters faced arrest and violence. Houses were bombed, police dogs attacked marchers, and civil rights workers were beaten and sometimes even killed.

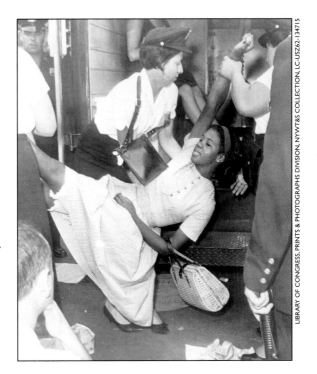

When civil rights protesters like this young woman were arrested, it brought attention to the movement.

sit-in: a protest in which people refuse to leave a business that discriminates   **rally**: a gathering of a large group of people for a specific cause   **registered**: officially signed up

Events of the civil rights movement were constantly on television and in the newspapers during those years. Even in the North, people heard about the marches, sit-ins, and boycotts going on in the South. They saw pictures of bloody protesters and heard stories of discrimination. As a result, more people from the North, including many white people, began to support the civil rights movement.

Starting in 1961, Father Groppi got involved. He made several trips to the South with Catholics and other **clergy** members, as well as northern civil rights **activists**. Other activists from the North, including many in the clergy, made similar trips. They believed the Bible said that equality was everyone's right and that they should speak out against injustice. Father Groppi's **superiors** in the Catholic Church supported his work, seeing it as part of the church's **mission** of helping the poor and those in need.

clergy (**klur** jee): the people trained to lead a religious group, such as priests and rabbis
activist: someone who works to produce political or social change   **superior**: someone with a higher rank or position than others   **mission** (**mish** uhn): a particular task given to a person or group to carry out

Civil Rights Protests

Civil rights activists tried to change society in many different ways. They led marches, sent around **petitions**, and held sit-ins.

Sit-ins were common in the movement. Activists would go to a place that discriminated against black people. They would sit down and wait to be treated the same as white customers,

Taking part in a sit-in wasn't easy. These protesters had food dumped on them by people who disagreed with them.

blocking the area and stopping business or traffic. Often they were arrested or attacked. In the 1950s and early 1960s, famous sit-ins took place in Oklahoma City, Oklahoma; Nashville, Tennessee; and Greensboro, North Carolina, but the **tactic** was used hundreds of times around the country.

petition (puh **ti** shuhn): a letter signed by many people asking those in power to change a law or rule
tactic: a plan or method to achieve a goal

The Clergy in the Civil Rights Movement

Clergyman or *clergywoman* are words for an official leader from any religion. Priests, ministers, and rabbis are all members of the clergy. During the civil rights movement, members of the clergy from many different religions spoke out for equality. Father Groppi marched with other Catholic priests, pastors, nuns, and Jewish rabbis. Martin Luther King Jr. was a minister, as were many other civil rights workers around him, including Jesse Jackson

and Ralph Abernathy. Many white clergy members supported civil rights, although others spoke out against the movement.

LIBRARY OF CONGRESS, PRINTS & PHOTOGRAPHS DIVISION, LC-USZ6-23292

Many religious people joined the civil rights movement, working together to achieve equality for all people.

On these trips to the South, Father Groppi saw **extreme** examples of discrimination and suffering in the black community. He didn't just watch, though. He worked with activists to integrate segregated restaurants, and he helped black people register to vote. He faced the same dangers that southern civil rights workers faced, and he was inspired by the courage he saw in people.

At the time, it was illegal in Mississippi and other states to allow blacks and whites to eat together in restaurants. On one of his trips south, Father Groppi sat in a restaurant in Mississippi with Peggy, a black civil rights worker, and Nathaniel, a black friend from Wisconsin.

Father Groppi remembered that as the 3 of them sat drinking coffee and talking, "a white fellow got up and walked to the other side of the counter. A group of white men began to gather behind me. I paid the bill and we were followed outside and across the street." Father Groppi tried to ignore the white men and stay calm. If he challenged them, he thought they might attack.

extreme (ek **streem**): very great

35

"I got into the car very slowly," he said. "But Peggy became nervous, and she began to scream, 'Start the car, start the car!'"

When they returned to the civil rights office, Nathaniel said, "Man, I was afraid, but not Father. He was perfectly calm."

"But I was afraid," replied Father Groppi. He just hadn't let his fear show.

On the same trip with Nathaniel to Tennessee, something similar happened. The 2 of them were driving past a factory. The white workers saw a black man and a white man together in a car. "They chased us down the highway," Father Groppi recalled. "I am telling you, I was afraid. I took out my **rosary** and I prayed from Memphis [Tennessee] to Jackson [Mississippi] without stopping. We didn't stop. You couldn't go to the bathroom. . . . You were afraid to stop to get something to eat."

Father Groppi's rosary

rosary (**roh** suh ree): a string of beads that Catholics use to count out prayers

36

As Father Groppi saw how southern blacks lived, he became more and more angry at their situation. He saw how black people were **denied** jobs and good educations. He saw the terrible houses they lived in, and he heard about the violence blacks faced from racists. He felt the **atmosphere** of fear and **poverty**, and he knew he had to work for racial justice.

Blacks in the South often lived in very poor houses, like these ones in Tennessee.

At the time, most people thought of the South as the home of discrimination and prejudice. But Father Groppi realized that many of the same things were happening right where he lived in Milwaukee. Every day he saw how black

denied: not allowed   **atmosphere** (**at** muh sfir): the mood or feeling of a place   **poverty**: the state of being poor

people faced discrimination in his own parish in the North. He began to wonder how he could fight for equality at home.

In 1963, Father Groppi attended the March on Washington, where Dr. King gave his famous "I Have a Dream" speech. Dr. King, who was the most well-known leader of the civil rights movement, inspired him. But Father Groppi knew

The famous March on Washington brought as many as 300,000 people to Washington, DC.

that thousands of other activists who were not famous were working just as hard, taking risks and facing violence. He was **determined** to do his part in working for justice.

He said, "What happened was that as you went along in the movement, you got swallowed up in the cause. And the cause was the cause of **righteousness**. Pretty soon your fear was gone. Nothing mattered anymore. The cause **consumed** you and the cause was more important than your life."

There was no turning back for Father Groppi. He was deeply committed to the civil rights movement.

---

determined: strongly wanting to do something   **righteousness** (rɪ chus nis): moral goodness or rightness
consumed: had your full attention

5

Selma

Father Groppi mostly took part in the civil rights struggle during his summer vacation. But in 1965, his commitment took a giant leap forward when he went to Selma, Alabama.

Martin Luther King Jr.

Since 1963, civil rights workers had been trying to organize black voters in and around Selma. Only 130 of the county's 15,000 black people were registered to vote. Community leaders **intimidated** blacks to keep them from registering. In 1965, organizers asked Martin Luther King Jr. to help. He agreed to hold a march from Selma to Montgomery, Alabama's capital, to call attention to the problem.

On March 7, 1965, Dr. King started from Selma with around 600 marchers. They only got as far as the Pettus Bridge, 6 blocks away. Local and state police troopers stopped the peaceful protesters with **billy clubs**, whips, and **tear gas**. Marchers were beaten and bloodied.

Pettus Bridge in Selma, Alabama

intimidated: frightened or threatened   **billy club**: a short, thin club often used by police   **tear gas**: a gas that causes pain and irritation in the eyes, often used to break up crowds

Blocking the Vote

Southern **authorities** knew that if many black people voted, they would gain power and be able to change laws. There were many ways to keep blacks from voting. Some states charged a **poll** tax to vote. Because many black people were poor, they couldn't pay and couldn't vote. Other places made voters take tests to be able to vote. Only blacks were tested, and the tests were very difficult. Many blacks in the South were not well educated and could not pass such tests. Other times, blacks were simply threatened with violence if they went to the polls on Election Day.

It was important for African Americans to vote so they could gain power and be able to change laws.

National television stations and major newspapers showed shocking images of the violence. People all over the country

authority: someone in charge who has a lot of power, such as a politician   **poll**: the place where people go to vote

were stunned by what they saw. Martin Luther King Jr. asked activists from the North and South to come to Selma and show their support. He held a short second march on March 9, but stopped to wait for a court to decide if the march could go forward **legally**. During this time, more activists arrived in Selma.

On March 12, Father Groppi and several other priests and nuns traveled south to support the third march. They waited in Selma for the march to begin, living in a **housing project** with local people.

Although this group from Wisconsin had been told to stay together for their own safety when walking through Selma, Father Groppi didn't listen. He kept wandering off on his own. One of the priests who traveled with him said, "One minute he would be there, the next minute he would be gone—down a dusty side street **heedless** of his own safety, to sit on a **rickety** porch or in the dust of a grassless yard to play with the little black children. Few shied away from him." Father Groppi wanted to learn about the lives of the people in Selma. He was

---

legally: in a way that is allowed by law   **housing project**: a group of buildings built by the government to give poor people an affordable place to live   **heedless**: not paying attention to something   **rickety**: poorly made and likely to fall apart

good at making connections with the black people who lived there, and he was not afraid.

Civil rights activists taught the newcomers to face the dangers of protesting in the South. Protesters were trained in tactics of **nonviolent civil disobedience**. In Selma, Father Groppi learned to link arms, dodge rocks, endure taunts and violence, and overcome fear.

Nonviolent Civil Disobedience

Civil disobedience is a way of changing society by breaking unfair laws on purpose. In American history, protesters have often chosen to break laws they thought were unfair. In 1773, the Boston Tea Party organizers showed their opposition to unfair taxes by illegally dumping tea into Boston harbor. Before the Civil War, those who disagreed with slavery hid runaway slaves illegally. In the early 1900s, women who wanted the right to vote chained themselves to the White House fence.

The civil rights movement took part in this tradition of civil disobedience. When Rosa Parks was arrested for not giving up her seat on the bus, she was practicing civil disobedience. It was

nonviolent civil disobedience: refusing to follow laws and not fighting back when arrested, with the goal of getting the government to change the way things are

against the law for her to stay in her seat, but she knew the law was unjust, so she stayed where she was.

Protesters who practice civil disobedience break the law, and then accept consequences like going to jail or being fined. By breaking the law, they draw attention to the way in which the law is unfair or unjust. Marches, **picketing**, protests, and sit-ins can all be forms of civil disobedience. Father Groppi and his friends Nathaniel and Peggy practiced civil disobedience when they ate together in the restaurant in Mississippi.

WHI IMAGE ID 52893

Civil disobedience is also nonviolent. Protesters pledge not to fight back if attacked. Facing violence without responding helps to gain sympathy for a cause. When television viewers saw marchers

Rosa Parks's civil disobedience helped change unjust laws and encouraged the civil rights movement.

picketing: standing outside a place to protest, usually with signs

being beaten in Selma and not fighting back, support for the civil rights movement rose.

It takes great courage not to fight back or use violence against unjust laws. Not all civil rights protests were peaceful. In some cities, **riots** and violence broke out. Between 1963 and 1968, there were large riots in cities like Detroit, Los Angeles, Atlanta, San Francisco, and New York.

On another day in Selma, Father Groppi heard that some activists had been attacked by **white supremacists** in Montgomery. He and 5 other clergymen got into a car and began to race down the highway toward Montgomery to see how they could help. A police car followed them for several miles, so they slowed down and made sure they didn't give the police a reason to pull them over. Local police often **harassed** civil rights activists by arresting them to keep them from being part of **demonstrations**. Eventually, the police car pulled away, and Father Groppi sped up again, all the way to Montgomery.

---

riot (rı uht): a violent and disordered group of people   **white supremacist** (suh **prem** uh sist): a person who believes the white race is better than any other   **harassed**: bothered or annoyed repeatedly
demonstration: a public gathering in which people show feelings for or against something

White Supremacy

White supremacists believe that the white race is better than all other races. White supremacy is a form of racism and prejudice. The Ku Klux Klan is the most well-known organization of white supremacists in the United States. In the civil rights struggle, many white supremacists attacked, beat, and even killed civil rights activists, and the Ku Klux Klan planted bombs at civil rights offices. White supremacists and their organizations, including the Ku Klux Klan, still exist in the United States today.

When they arrived in Montgomery, the clergymen attended a church meeting with Martin Luther King Jr. and other leaders. The air was filled with **tension**. One observer said the old church "was so packed that some people were **literally** hanging from the **rafters**." When Dr. King stepped onto the stage to speak, the roar made by the audience "almost lifted the roof off. It was like standing near the exhaust of a jet airliner."

tension: a feeling of nervousness, stress, or suspense   **literally**: in actual fact and not exaggerated
rafter: a beam that supports a roof

After the meeting, some of the religious leaders marched to the capitol building. State police troopers blocked their way. Father Groppi and his group wanted to offer a prayer on the capitol steps. The state troopers finally allowed it.

As he prayed, Father Groppi said that all people are part of one family, with a responsibility to help each other. He added, "If we go to church on Sunday and preach . . . and then do nothing . . . we are **hypocrites**."

Father Groppi and his Wisconsin companions had to return home before the third march began on March 21. But more than 8,000 people were in the third march, which successfully reached Montgomery on March 25.

Many historians see the march from Selma as a turning point in the civil rights movement. When pictures of police beating marchers were shown on television and in newspapers, people everywhere could see how strong racism was in the South. People saw how southern states maintained segregation and discrimination through **brutality**

hypocrite (**hip** uh krit): a person who claims to believe something but whose actions don't match that belief
brutality: violent cruelty

LIBRARY OF CONGRESS, PRINTS & PHOTOGRAPHS DIVISION, LC-USZ62-133090

More than 8,000 people joined the third march from Selma to Montgomery.

and intimidation. Public opinion began to change in favor of new laws to ban discrimination.

Father Groppi returned to Wisconsin with his group, but Selma had changed him. Although he saw the importance of being part of the civil rights struggle in the South, he also decided that he could do something in his own state and city. Milwaukee had plenty of racial discrimination that he could **confront**, and he was determined to do just that.

confront: deal with something directly

But not everyone who went to the South with him agreed. "I wasn't the only white minister or priest from Milwaukee who went down to join King's movement," he said. "There were five or six others. But when I asked some of them to join me in protesting against discrimination in Milwaukee, they just couldn't find it in themselves to do it. Their wives and relatives and neighbors live here. It's one thing to go down south and protest against injustice, but don't start to do it in your own backyard."

Father Groppi could see that they didn't want to challenge the people they knew and saw every day. It was easier to challenge people far away whom they would probably never see again.

Father Groppi knew that the issues of equality and justice were important in his neighborhood, not just in Mississippi or Alabama. Soon after his return from Selma, he said, "In the South there is a constant working to **overcome**. This is something we need to learn in the North. **Bigotry** is not confined to any one state. It is present here in Wisconsin."

overcome: to deal with or get past a problem or challenge   **bigotry**: prejudice

50

Many people understood the problems of racism. But Father Groppi was determined not only to understand the problems but also to do something. He wanted to change things not just in states a thousand miles away, but also right where he lived, in Milwaukee.

6

Becoming a Milwaukee Organizer

When Father Groppi returned from Selma in March 1965, he looked for ways to be involved in civil rights activism in Wisconsin. He had seen civil rights organizers arrested in the South, and whether he knew it or not, he would soon be arrested himself for protesting discrimination.

In Milwaukee at that time, students went to schools in their own neighborhoods. Since black and white people didn't live close to each other, they didn't go to the same schools. Nearly 20 schools were mostly black, while all the other schools in Milwaukee had very few, if any, black students. Even though there weren't laws keeping the students in separate schools like in the South, there was still segregation. Since 1963, civil rights activists had tried to end segregation in Milwaukee schools by talking with the **school board**, but nothing had changed.

school board: the group of people in charge of a public school district

United States law said that schools had to be **desegregated** so that education would be fair for everyone. The Milwaukee School District decided to deal with the problem of segregation through a **policy** of busing, which other cities were also trying.

School Segregation

Why were segregated schools bad? Why not just let black and white students go to separate schools in their own neighborhoods?

On May 17, 1954, the US Supreme Court decided a historic case called *Brown v. the Board of Education*. This legal ruling said that having separate public schools for black and white students was illegal and that segregation in education must end. The court said that even if school

The Supreme Court decided that segregation in education must end.

desegregated: made to be no longer segregated   policy (**pol** uh see): plan of action

buildings were equal, students of one race who were made to stay apart from students of another race would feel inferior and discriminated against. And this meant that their education wouldn't be as good.

In reality, segregated school buildings weren't equal anyway. The white students got the better schools. Schools that taught black students in Milwaukee were older, were in worse condition, and often lacked good equipment or books. Separate was not the same as equal.

African American students from overcrowded inner-city schools were loaded onto buses that took them to schools in white neighborhoods. However, these inner-city students were kept away from the white students. They were in different rooms with separate teachers. Sometimes these students were bused back to their own neighborhood to eat. Black and white students didn't even share the same lunchroom! Although black and white students were in the same buildings, this kind of busing was just segregation in disguise.

On May 18, 1964, a group called the Milwaukee United School Integration **Committee**, known as MUSIC, led a boycott of Milwaukee schools to protest segregation and the busing policy.

Boycotts

Boycotts are a way of drawing attention to problems or injustice by refusing to deal with an organization or business. Protesters agree not to buy certain products or go to certain businesses. When these businesses lose money, they may change their policies or support the goals of the protesters.

Rosa Parks's refusal to give up her seat led to a boycott of the bus system in Montgomery. When black people didn't ride the buses, the bus company lost money, which created pressure for change. In order to bring customers back and make money, they had to change their policy. Sometimes boycotts are intended to hurt a company financially, and other times they simply draw public attention to a problem.

MUSIC urged black students to stay away from school for a day. The activists set up "freedom schools" around the city so students would have somewhere else to go during the

committee (kuh **mit** ee): a group of people chosen to meet about a topic and make a decision

boycott. Over half of all the black students in the Milwaukee school system did not attend school that day.

Most of the freedom schools were held in churches or private homes. In these schools, **volunteer** teachers taught students regular subjects, but they also taught about African

Activists set up "freedom schools" around Milwaukee so students could still learn.

volunteer: someone who offers to do something without getting paid for it

history and customs. The leaders wanted students to learn about and be proud of their **heritage**.

Through the spring of 1965, civil rights activists continued to talk with the school board, but nothing changed. When Father Groppi returned from Selma, he joined MUSIC.

In May and June, MUSIC members began to picket and block school buses to protest segregation. Some of them were arrested. MUSIC released a statement that said the demonstrations were a warning. "We will continue picketing, sit-ins, lay-ins, chain-ins and any other kind of 'in' until the . . . school board caves in," they wrote. "Apparently, they won't do anything on their own . . . so we will have to **persuade** them."

On June 4, 1965, Father Groppi was arrested with 4 other clergymen as they formed a **human chain** in front of a school bus. This was the first time he had been arrested for civil disobedience. He and his friends were each fined 10 dollars.

Three days after his arrest, Father Groppi spoke at a rally. "I believe that a clergyman's place is with his people," he said.

heritage (**hair** uh tij): traditions and culture passed on by ancestors   **persuade** (per **swayd**): convince
human chain: a group of people tightly holding on to each other's arms so that they form a line that can't be easily broken

57

MUSIC members picketed and blocked school buses to protest segregation.

"There have been 10 of my **parishioners** who submitted themselves to arrest to point out what they believe was an injustice." Father Groppi didn't think they should have to go to jail alone.

Father Groppi went on to say that people should try legal means, like voting or talking, to change unfair laws. But if those ways didn't work, people had a right to break the laws. Activists might face arrest and violence if they did this, but

parishioner: a member of a parish

58

they should be willing to live with the consequences. Activists could draw attention to the unfair laws and show their own commitment to changing them, which might change other people's minds as well.

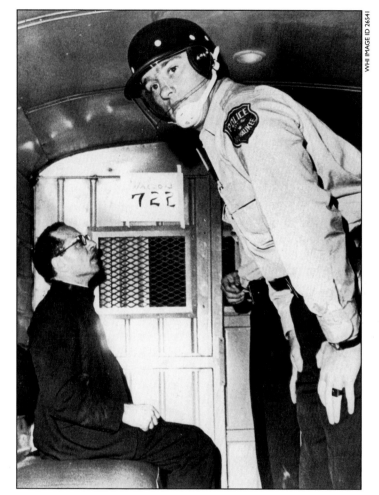

Father Groppi in a police van after getting arrested

This was the first time Father Groppi had spoken out so publicly. He attracted attention for his speech. Soon afterward, he was asked to be the youth advisor for the Wisconsin NAACP. He was responsible for helping young members decide how they could work to change racist attitudes and laws. He also helped run meetings to make sure that members were working together and listening to each other.

The NAACP

The National Association for the Advancement of Colored People (NAACP) was founded in 1909. Its mission is "to **ensure** the political, educational, social, and **economic** equality of rights of all persons and to **eliminate** racial hatred and racial discrimination." It is one of the oldest and most powerful civil rights organizations in the United States. Its name is one of the last surviving formal uses of the term *colored people* for African Americans.

The NAACP was formed to fight for equality for all people.

---

ensure (en **shur**): make certain that something happens   **economic** (ee kah **nahm** ik): having to do with the way a place runs its industry, trade, and finance   **eliminate**: get rid of

School segregation continued, and MUSIC leaders announced that they would boycott the schools again in October. Although judges and **politicians** tried to stop the boycott, thousands of students stayed out of school, again attending freedom schools.

Church officials did not support the movement or MUSIC. They ordered priests not to use their churches for freedom schools. Father Groppi and other priests wrote a letter saying that they would obey the church, even though they disagreed.

When the boycott began on Monday morning, 500 children and parents showed up at the doors of St. Boniface Catholic Church. They thought there would be a freedom school there. Father Groppi met them at the door. He couldn't allow them to come into the building, so he led them to a local **Baptist** church.

That night, more than 200 people returned to his church, expecting there to be a rally. Again, Father Groppi led them to another church. The protesters decided to march to the home of the Milwaukee School Board director, John Foley, which was several miles away. They wanted to talk directly to him and tell him what they wanted to change in the schools.

politician (pol uh **tish** uhn): someone who runs for or holds public office, such as a senator **Baptist**: a large Christian group in the United States

Father Groppi led the march. Along the way, the marchers showed how much they respected him. When the group reached Foley's home, they were making a lot of noise. The police threatened to arrest them if they weren't quiet. When Father Groppi asked, all of the **demonstrators** became silent. He

WHI IMAGE ID 4993

You're never too young to stand up for what you believe in, as this young protester proves.

said, "We have made our point. Now we will march back to St. Boniface in prayerful silence." They did, without any problems.

demonstrator: someone taking part in a demonstration

Father Groppi had calmed a situation that might have become violent, and he kept the demonstrators from getting arrested.

After the march, church officials banned Father Groppi from participating in the boycott. He disagreed, but he

The protesters decided to march with Father Groppi to the home of the Milwaukee School Board director.

obeyed his superiors. It was the last time he was ordered not to be involved in civil rights work.

Soon after the boycott, the school district began to build a new school in Milwaukee's black neighborhood. The district said that this new school would improve education for black students. MUSIC leaders saw that the new school would still be segregated even if it were a better building. They began to protest at the construction site, and Father Groppi was arrested again, along with many other clergy members, for blocking a gate.

The protests didn't work. Segregation continued. After more than 2 years, MUSIC gave up in **frustration**. They held one last march from the construction site to the school **administration** building, 38 blocks away. Again, Father Groppi was in front. A Milwaukee newspaper called him "a leader in civil rights demonstrations."

frustration: a feeling of helplessness and discouragement   **administration**: having to do with the leading and managing of a group

Desegregating Milwaukee Schools

The road to desegregation was long and slow. When the protests didn't work, organizers tried a different approach. In 1965, Lloyd Barbee, a MUSIC organizer, filed a lawsuit to desegregate Milwaukee schools. Eleven years later, in 1976, the courts finally agreed and ordered the schools desegregated.

Lloyd Barbee, a MUSIC organizer, filed the lawsuit that eventually desegregated Milwaukee schools.

The campaign had not changed the Milwaukee schools. It had not ended segregation. However, it had received a lot of news **coverage**. The school campaign wasn't the only thing that received coverage. Suddenly, Father Groppi was a well-known public figure. He was famous in Milwaukee, and his name began to be known around the country.

coverage (**kuhv** ur ij): attention

65

7

The Eagles Club Protests

Soon after the MUSIC school boycott ended, the Milwaukee NAACP Youth **Council** asked Father Groppi to be their advisor. The Youth Council was a group of black people in Milwaukee dedicated to civil rights. They were connected to the larger NAACP but specifically worked for young people. Since he was already youth advisor for the state organization, it made sense for Father Groppi to have this role in Milwaukee as well.

Even though Father Groppi was white, the Youth Council thought he was the right person to help them. One member of the Youth Council put it this way: "He was really just right on the money in terms of what the problems were in the community and wanting to do something. He was feeling like [we] were feeling, like what direction are we going to go? What are we going to *do*? How do we start this?"

council (**cown** suhl): a group of people who run an organization

WHI IMAGE ID 53596

Father Groppi and the Milwaukee NAACP Youth Council

The Youth Council was **democratic**. Nine chosen officers voted on actions. Father Groppi simply offered them ideas, although they often followed his advice. One member said, "The only time he'd say something in the ... meeting was if somebody asked him for his opinion. Otherwise, he'd sit and listen."

The members of the council didn't want to just sit and talk, though. They wanted to do something. "When it was

democratic (dem uh **krat** ik): making decision by vote, with everyone having an equal say

a question of whether we should act or not, we acted," said Father Groppi.

Members of the Youth Council had been involved in the MUSIC school protests. They were disappointed that schools hadn't changed, so they were looking for another way to challenge segregation and discrimination. They found a new target in the Eagles Club of Milwaukee.

Who Are the Eagles?

The **Fraternal** Order of Eagles was started in 1898 in Seattle, Washington. It is a social club where members can enjoy activities and relax. The Eagles also help charities and work for the improvement of communities. Many politicians, including 7 US presidents, have been members, as well as many popular entertainers and sports figures. The Eagles also started the celebration of Mother's Day in the United States.

Early in 1966, a member of St. Boniface told the Youth Council that he could not go swimming at the Eagles Club because he was black. He said, "They're making me feel

fraternal: having to do with brothers or humanity generally

68

like there is something wrong with me." The Youth Council replied that it was the Eagles Club that had something wrong with it, because it was discriminating. The Youth Council decided they would push the Eagles Club to let black people be members.

In 1966, the Milwaukee Eagles Club was the second largest in the nation. It had more than 5,400 members, including most of the city's politicians, judges, and business leaders. The Eagles were a private club, and they were legally free to choose members however they wanted. They were free to discriminate. Members could get to know important and powerful people in Milwaukee. Since black people could not join, they didn't have the same chance to get to know the city leaders as white people had. The Youth Council thought that was unfair.

The members of the Youth Council had to decide how to protest the Eagles' policy. Around the country, other activists had similar goals. They **targeted** organizations that practiced discrimination or segregation, trying to get them to open up

targeted: aimed at

their doors to everyone. Once one organization agreed to open membership, hopefully others would follow.

Some groups wanted to use violence and armed **revolution** to deal with discrimination, but Father Groppi and the Youth Council were committed to nonviolence. Father Groppi had learned about the importance of nonviolence from his time in the South. He believed in drawing attention to problems. He also believed that violence would only make people turn against civil rights workers.

The Youth Council wanted the Eagles Club to accept anyone as a member, but the Eagles refused. They said they could do whatever they wanted with their own membership policies. In February and March of 1966, Youth Council members began to picket the Eagles Club. They marched on the street, carrying signs and singing. No one paid much attention.

They continued their protests until August, when a bomb set by Ku Klux Klan members blew up the office of the Milwaukee NAACP. The bomb wasn't aimed at the Eagles

revolution: the overthrow of a government or leader

The Youth Council picketed the Eagles Club.

Club protest directly, but it made further violence seem possible. Although no one was injured, the bombing increased the fear and tension around the protests.

The Youth Council decided to try a different approach. They wanted to get members to **resign** from the club in protest. If the Eagles wouldn't end their policy of segregation, the council thought that anyone in a powerful position in the city should give up his or her membership. They felt those who truly believed that all people were equal should have

resign: give up a position or job

71

PHOTOGRAPH COURTESY OF THE MILWAUKEE JOURNAL SENTINEL

Protesters marched on the street, carrying signs and singing.

nothing to do with segregated groups. If a politician or a judge was part of a club that was segregated, it seemed as if that person agreed with the idea of segregation. Could such a person be trusted to be fair?

They decided to picket at the home of one of the Eagles' members, Judge Robert Cannon. They wanted him to resign from the Eagles Club to protest against its policies. Judge Cannon had a **reputation** as a **liberal** judge because he often

reputation (rep yoo **tay** shun): a person's worth or character as judged by other people   **liberal**: in this case, someone who supported civil rights for all

supported civil rights. Father Groppi and his group thought that Judge Cannon was likely to agree with their cause.

Each evening, Father Groppi drove Youth Council members to **Wauwatosa**, a middle-class white **suburb** of Milwaukee, where they stood before Judge Cannon's home with signs. Angry white neighbors met them there. Some of these neighbors threw bottles, eggs, and **cherry bombs** as they shouted at the marchers, "Go back to the zoo!" and

PHOTOGRAPH COURTESY OF THE MILWAUKEE JOURNAL SENTINEL

Linking arms and singing helped the protesters stick together.

Wauwatosa: waw wuh **toh** suh   **suburb**: an area with homes and stores located outside the main area of a city
cherry bomb: a small explosive, like a firework

73

"Go back to the jungle!" These racist **slogans** implied that blacks were little more than animals and didn't belong where white people lived. They are a good example of racism and prejudice.

They also shouted at the police who were there to protect the marchers, saying, "Kill them!" and "White trash!" Other neighbors came to watch, and a concession stand even sold popcorn and soda.

Father Groppi was not the only clergyman involved, but he was the leader. Rabbi Stern, a local Jewish leader, said that the "Eagles were behaving more like vultures" by not changing their policies.

Nate Harwell was a Youth Council member at that time. He said of Judge Cannon, "We thought he would be one of the easiest guys because of his past civil rights record. Everybody has said how liberal he was."

The Youth Council was wrong. Judge Cannon refused to leave the Eagles Club. He said, "I want everyone in Milwaukee

slogan (**sloh** guhn): a phrase or motto

to know that I will . . . remain in the Eagles as long as I live. I may not agree with that policy, but if I resign, how can I work to get it changed?"

After 9 nights of protests, 400 National Guard troops came to protect the demonstrators. Two days later, the Youth Council agreed to meet with Eagles officials to discuss their issues.

That spring, Father Groppi started a place called the Freedom House in a building in one of Milwaukee's worst neighborhoods. He lived there with some of the Youth Council members.

Freedom House, the Youth Council headquarters

After the bombing of the NAACP office, some of the Youth Council members no longer felt safe. They feared that Freedom House might be the next target for a bombing.

Father Groppi complained that the police weren't protecting Freedom House well enough. He said that 2 officers had been seen sleeping and a third had asked for comic books to read. "We don't need this kind of protection," he said. "I believe in **self-defense**."

In October, as **negotiations** with the Eagles continued, Father Groppi and the Youth Council formed what they called a **commando** unit. It was made up of young black men who were trained to maintain order and protect demonstrators. These commandos wore uniforms of army pants, boots, and black **berets**. They seemed like a military unit.

The commandos started guarding Freedom House with a loaded gun. The thought of a house in Milwaukee's slums being guarded by armed youths was frightening to many white people. They feared that black people were preparing for a violent attack by training an army.

self-defense: the ability to fight back to protect yourself or the things you own
negotiation (ni goh shee **ay** shun): a discussion of something in order to come to an agreement
commando: a member of a military group **beret** (buh **ray**): a round, flat hat

Father Groppi said that the commando group was needed after the bombing of the NAACP office and the violence directed at Youth Council protesters. He also wanted to build **discipline** and pride among the commandos. But many white people were frightened by the idea of young black men acting like soldiers. They feared that the commandos would not merely protect demonstrators, but that they might also attack white people.

In response, the commandos said that their policy was "not violent." According to one commando leader, "Not violence meant we didn't carry weapons and we didn't start nothing, but we also didn't take nothing. If the police or the white crowds came after us, or the marchers, we weren't afraid to mix it up, to fight back."

The commandos protected people. One activist later said, "It was self-defense that kept most of those people from getting seriously hurt. If it wasn't for the **brute** strength and the **outgoing** nature of the men in the commandos at that time, the bulk of the people in those lines would have got hurt; somebody might have got killed."

discipline (**dis** uh plin): control over the way you act or behave   **brute**: physical rather than intellectual
outgoing: confident and willing to engage others

Members of the Youth Council had to be brave to stand their ground.

After negotiations with the Eagles went nowhere, the Youth Council stopped their protests. Once again, a civil rights campaign had not achieved its goals. In the end, a few Eagles members did resign, and the Eagles Club lost a little business because some people no longer held events at the club. But overall, not much changed either in Milwaukee or at the Eagles Club.

Although these protests, whether at the Eagles Club or against school desegregation, may not have been successful right away, in the long run they helped to change attitudes about segregation and discrimination. Today, no community leader would be part of a discriminatory club. This change is in part because of the many actions and demonstrations of the civil rights movement to draw attention to the problem. What may not have been successful in the short term still made an impact in the long run.

As a result of the Eagles Club protests, Father Groppi and the Youth Council changed. They felt **unified** and determined. They knew that they were part of a national movement, and they were still committed to equal rights. Even if the Eagles campaign was not a victory, Father Groppi and the Youth Council were ready to take on a new challenge. They would work to change unfair housing practices in Milwaukee.

unified: brought together as one, not many

8

The Fair Housing Campaign

Housing discrimination was common in the United States in the 1960s. A white person would refuse to rent or sell a home to a black person just because of the color of his or her skin. Some cities passed "fair housing" laws to fix the problem. These laws guaranteed all people the right to live where they wanted and made it illegal to turn down a buyer or renter because of skin color. Milwaukee did not have such a law.

In its early years, Milwaukee's black residents made up a small percentage of the total population. From 1920 through 1940, the African American population in Milwaukee grew, as people moved from the South to look for jobs. But these new arrivals often had a hard time finding good places to live. They faced discrimination in housing.

The Great Migration

The movement of black people to Milwaukee was part of a trend in US history called the Great **Migration**. Between 1910 and 1970, over 6 million African Americans moved from the South to the North and West. They came looking for work, but they were also trying to escape the discrimination they faced in the South. Northern cities had more jobs and better schools, and it was much easier for black people to vote.

African Americans also moved from farms and the countryside to cities. Large cities all over the

Because of the Great Migration, millions of African Americans began to live in cities.

country began to have neighborhoods with lots of black people, living all together in what were called **ghettos**. Because of housing discrimination, African Americans were forced to live in the older and run-down houses, and northern cities became segregated. The Great Migration changed the shape of the United States, but it didn't mean the end of discrimination.

migration (mɪ **gray** shuhn): movement from one community to another in the same country
ghetto (**get** oh): a usually poor city neighborhood where people of the same race, religion, or ethnic background live, often not by choice

Most black people lived in one part of Milwaukee's inner city that came to be called "the inner **core**." Houses there were old. Apartment buildings were often in bad shape. Even back in 1945, a study had said that the city was "dying at its core." In 1950, the *Milwaukee Journal* called this area "a **dilapidated**, overcrowded **tinder box**."

But no politicians or business leaders did anything to improve the situation. By the 1960s, conditions were even worse. But when black people tried to rent or buy homes outside of the inner core, they were met with **hostility** or simply turned away.

Black people wanted to live in better houses and better neighborhoods, but there was no law to protect their right to live wherever they chose. A landlord could discriminate, and no one could do anything about it. In some neighborhoods, homeowners signed agreements never to sell or rent to black people.

Ronald Britton was an ex-**Marine** who had served in Vietnam. Late in 1966, after the Eagles campaign ended, he

core: center or middle   **dilapidated** (duh **lap** uh day tid): run down and falling apart   **tinder box**: a box for holding tinder, which is something flammable that can be used to start a fire   **hostility**: strong feelings against someone   **Marine** (muh **reen**): a member of the US Marine Corps, a special branch of the navy

WHI IMAGE ID 23669

Discrimination in housing makes it hard for some people to find a good place to live.

came to Father Groppi. He said that when he and his wife tried to rent an apartment in a white neighborhood, the landlady had turned them down. She asked them, "What would my neighbors think?" She thought her neighbors would be upset with her if she rented an apartment to black people. Ronald Britton wanted the right to live wherever he liked, but discrimination made it impossible to move someplace better.

Father Groppi spoke to the Youth Council, and they agreed to support Ronald Britton. They began by going to the home of the landlady who had refused to rent to him. They sang Christmas carols at her house to draw attention to her actions. But she didn't change her mind.

Other people were also working for fair housing. One of them was Vel Phillips, the first African American elected to Milwaukee's city council, which was called the Common Council. In 1962, she introduced a fair housing **ordinance** that said landlords could not discriminate in whom they rented houses to. She was

Vel Phillips wanted to pass a law to prevent discrimination in housing.

ordinance: a law issued by a government

84

the only one on the city council who voted in favor of it. She tried to pass the law several times over the next few years without any success. Father Groppi asked Vel Phillips if the Youth Council could work to get the fair housing law passed, and she was glad to have their help.

In June and July of 1967, the Youth Council started to picket at the homes and offices of **aldermen** who represented black neighborhoods. These same aldermen had voted against Mrs. Phillips's fair housing ordinance every time she introduced it. At some homes, more than 100 people picketed at a time. The aldermen either refused to speak to the protesters, or they tried to **defend** their votes against the ordinance.

In late July, Vel Phillips asked Father Groppi to speak to the Common Council about fair housing. The Common Council usually didn't allow unelected people to speak at their meetings, but the situation was becoming tense. They hoped that Father Groppi could help calm the community.

alderman: a neighborhood representative   **defend**: support or argue for

The Youth Council picketed at the homes and offices of aldermen.

archbishop: the highest-ranking priest in a city or other large area

Father Groppi warned that black people in the inner core were becoming angrier. They couldn't find good housing, and public officials were doing nothing. He warned that violence might follow, since peaceful protests weren't working.

One alderman became so upset with Father Groppi that he demanded that **Archbishop** Cousins, Father Groppi's superior, send him to Panama! News reports said that "his shouts could be heard throughout the **city clerk's** and aldermen's offices." The alderman was so angry that he tore a reporter's microphone from its cord. Tempers were rising on both sides of the issue.

Fair housing marchers

Tempers were also rising around the country. Many American cities experienced violent encounters between whites and blacks. Some were small, but others led to huge

city clerk: a public official who records important information about a city

87

riots. Many people wondered if, or when, Milwaukee would also explode into racial violence.

Five days after Father Groppi spoke to the city council, a **confrontation** between police and some black teenagers led to violence in the inner-core area. It was a small riot. Buildings were set on fire, and gunshots echoed through the night. More than 1,700 people were arrested and 3 people died.

The mayor feared that the whole city might explode in a huge riot. He declared a **curfew**, saying that for 10 days no one could be on Milwaukee streets at night. He also called in the National Guard to maintain order in case of further violence.

After the curfew ended, the National Guard left. A few weeks later, on August 23, the Youth Council announced that they would begin a new strategy to promote fair housing. They would lead a march into the white neighborhoods south of the Menomonee River. They wanted to demand the right for black people to live anywhere.

confrontation: a tense or violent meeting   **curfew** (**kur** fyoo): an order for people not to be outside after a certain time

9
Across the Great Divide

On August 28, 1967, more than 100 marchers gathered at the Freedom House on Fifteenth Street. They marched

through the streets and then south across the Sixteenth Street Viaduct. On the north side of the viaduct, around 50 white people from the south side, mostly from Father Groppi's old church, St. Veronica, held signs that said, "We South Siders Welcome Negroes."

WHI IMAGE ID 25167

Father Groppi and marchers on their way to the south side

The Longest Bridge in the World

The inner core was on the north side of the Menomonee River. Neighborhoods on the south side of the river were mostly white. Four long bridges, called viaducts, crossed the river. One of those bridges crossed the river at Sixteenth Street. Milwaukee residents used to say that the Sixteenth Street Viaduct was the longest bridge in the world, because it connected Africa and Poland. They said this because mostly black people lived on the north side and mostly Polish people lived on the south side.

The marchers crossed the long viaduct, looking down on the railroad yards, factories, and piles of coal that filled the valley alongside the river below them. They sang freedom songs to give themselves courage.

When they reached the south end of the viaduct, a very different greeting met them. Milwaukee police held back more than 3,000 angry white south-siders who held signs and yelled at the marchers.

Freedom Songs

During the civil rights struggle, protesters often sang together to create **unity** and strength as they faced violence and intimidation. Many of these freedom songs came from **spirituals** sung in black churches. These songs include "Oh, Freedom," "If You Miss Me at the Back of the Bus," and the most famous of the freedom songs, "We Shall Overcome."

Singing freedom songs together helped to create unity and strength.

The marchers were frightened, but they continued walking 3 miles to **Kosciuszko** Park. They planned to have a picnic there, since they didn't have a permit for a rally. By the time they arrived, more than 5,000 white people opposed to the march were gathered around the park, trying to **disrupt** the marchers.

unity (**yoo** ni tee): a feeling of agreement   **spiritual** (**spir** uh choo uhl): a type of religious folk song created by African Americans in the South   **Kosciuszko**: kosh **choo** skoh   **disrupt**: disturb or interrupt

Father Groppi attempted to speak, but the police urged the marchers to return to the north side. The police didn't think that they could hold back the angry crowd for long. After only 15 minutes, Father Groppi led the marchers away, but he said, "We're coming back tomorrow night. We want our picnic area."

They marched toward the viaduct. Hundreds of people followed them, shouting racist slogans like "We want our slaves!" as if black people should be returned to **captivity**. They chanted, "E-I-E-I-O, Father Groppi's got to go," showing their hatred of him.

Police protected the marchers as best they could. But when they reached the south end of the Sixteenth Street Viaduct, some south-siders had blocked the street with an old **hearse**. The hearse had a sign on it that said, "Father Groppi's Last Ride." The angry crowd began to throw bottles, rocks, and garbage. Some marchers held signs over their

captivity: the state of being held or kept without freedom   **hearse** (hurs): a car that carries a coffin during a funeral

heads for protection, while others ran for safety. Police fired tear gas at the violent south-side protesters, who began to **disperse**. Father Groppi and his marchers headed back over the viaduct.

The protesters had to be brave when marching into the south side. What would you have done in their situation?

disperse (**dis** purs): scatter

Later the next day, Father Groppi called the events a "white riot." He asked for the protection of the National Guard, because the marchers had a right to speak out and gather for their cause.

The next night, more people showed up on both sides. More than 12,000 south-siders waited for Father Groppi and about 200 marchers from the north side. There were more

Police officers guarding the marchers

police officers, as well as reporters from television stations and newspapers.

At first, the marchers were left alone as they crossed into the south side. The south-siders just held signs and yelled things. Father Groppi tried to keep the marchers calm. He said, "Keep cool. Walk fast. Girls in the middle. Don't be afraid. If we were afraid to die, we wouldn't be good Christians." The marchers kept going, protected by police and Youth Council commandos.

However, a few blocks from the park, a mob of people attacked. They carried signs that said "White Power." A reporter later said that the crowd, including teenagers and young children, chanted "kill, kill, kill, kill," over and over again. One young boy, maybe 3 years old, wore a sweatshirt that said "Go Home." The mob surrounded the police and the marchers.

The police fired tear gas at the white demonstrators, who scattered. However, the marchers were in bad shape. They suffered from tear gas, and many had been hurt by thrown objects or attacks.

The police tried to persuade Father Groppi to turn around, but he refused. "We'll stay here until the National Guard comes and we can march like free American citizens," he said. They intended to march to the park. The police **reluctantly** agreed and continued to protect the marchers, who began to sing the freedom song "Ain't Gonna Let Nobody Turn Me Around."

When they reached the park, Father Groppi spoke. He reminded marchers of their goal of fair housing and noted the strength they had shown so far. He said, "You've shown that you are willing to die for freedom." He inspired them to keep moving. They began to march back toward the viaduct. Again they were hit with bottles, eggs, and garbage, while firecrackers exploded around them. Some of the marchers were bloody and bruised, and many of them were **dazed** by tear gas and fear.

When the marchers returned to Freedom House, they were angry that the police had not protected them better. Tensions were high. The police wanted the marchers to

reluctantly: not wanting to do something   **dazed** (dayzd): stunned and unable to think clearly

96

PHOTOGRAPH COURTESY OF THE MILWAUKEE COUNTY HISTORICAL SOCIETY

Father Groppi spoke to the crowd when they reached the park.

disperse. When they didn't, the police fired tear gas into the house. The building caught fire and burned to the ground.

One activist, Betty Martin, recalled that night as "one of the most frightening experiences" of her life. "[To] not know if you are going to get out alive or not because you have never experienced anger like you had experienced it by going across that viaduct, and then to be pinned down with fire going over your head, with [police] actually shooting over your head at the Freedom House, and then . . . the house catching on fire."

The mayor banned all marches at night for 30 days. Father Groppi decided to respect the ban and not march the next night. When marchers gathered for a meeting in the ruins of Freedom House, police arrested more than 50 of them. People were angry, and the possibility of violence was strong.

Freedom House after it caught fire

❧

The following night, a Thursday, the Youth Council decided that they would march anyway, and Father Groppi changed his mind as well. They thought that the ban on marching was **unconstitutional**, and they were **eager** to act. A large group decided to march to City Hall, to see the mayor. But before they reached City Hall, more than 100 of them, including Father Groppi and Vel Phillips, were arrested for **defying** the ban.

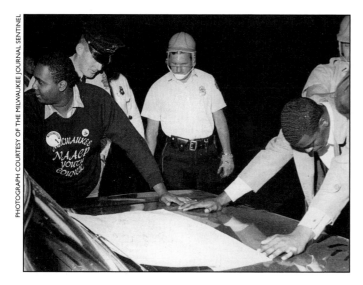

Marchers stood up for what they believed in, even when it meant they were arrested.

The next day, the mayor said that the ban on marching would end on Saturday, even though it was originally supposed to have lasted for 30 days. The marchers decided to

unconstitutional: against the rules described in the US Constitution   eager: interested and excited
defying: refusing to obey

disobey and march on Friday. They were immediately stopped by police, who arrested Father Groppi and others again.

The marches received national attention. Supporters arrived from around the country. On Saturday, more than 1,000 people marched to City Hall and through the south side. One week later, on September 10, at least 5,000 people marched to support fair housing.

One marcher remembered crossing the viaduct. "First thing, I was scared. Crossing the bridge seemed like it took forever. As we got closer and closer to National Street, you could hear them. You could hear the echo. You could hear the chants of 'White Power.' . . . We knew that the police weren't going to protect us. So, we cupped arm in arm. Everybody was really snug that first time we went over, sort of like a snake winding, and the closer we got, the more scared I got. . . . The first time was a lot of glass being thrown, beer bottles. . . . We couldn't march on the sidewalks anymore and had to go into the street. That's when most people got hurt."

Marches continued every day through the fall and winter. Sometimes there were violent confrontations and arrests, and sometimes the marches were peaceful.

People continued to march even though they faced violence.

Usually the violence came from the white protesters, who sometimes used racist language and images. On Sunday and Monday, September 10 and 11, white mobs fought police,

101

who needed tear gas to disperse them. These crowds threw
firecrackers, bottles, and bricks. They chanted slogans like "We
Want Slaves," and held signs that said, "Block Them Off, Nobody
Goes South." One sign said, "Open Housing in Africa," meaning
that blacks could have fair housing—if they went back to
Africa.

The anti-fair housing protesters made fiery speeches too.
"We're setting up the platform for a White Power march . . . to
the jungle where Groppi operates," said one speaker. "We're
going to end the black **scourge**." Although many people used
such language then, it was clearly racist.

One Monday night, the violence was so intense that the fair
housing marchers ran back north across the viaduct. Father
Groppi said, "If we had gone any further, they would have
slaughtered us."

At the height of the protests, Martin Luther King Jr. sent
Father Groppi a **telegram**. "What you and your courageous
associates are doing in Milwaukee will certainly serve as a kind
of massive nonviolence that we need in this **turbulent** period.

scourge (skurj): a source of wide-ranging and great problems.   **slaughtered** (slaw turd): killed many people
telegram: a message that is sent by telegraph   **associate** (uh **soh** see it): someone working with another
person   **turbulent**: wild, confused, or violent

You are demonstrating that it is possible to be **militant** and powerful without destroying life or property. Please know that you have my support and prayers."

While the marches continued, activists also boycotted local **breweries** and stores. They started a "Black Christmas" project, in which people would not buy things for Christmas from local businesses. If local businesses lost money, perhaps they would support equal rights in order to bring customers back. Activists were using every tactic they could think of to bring fair housing to Milwaukee.

The city council still refused to pass a fair housing law, but by spring, communities around Milwaukee began to pass such laws. In late March 1968, Father Groppi and the NAACP Youth Council ended the protests after 200 days of marches in a row. But there still wasn't a fair housing law in Milwaukee. They had not accomplished what they had hoped for.

A few days later, on April 4, Dr. Martin Luther King Jr. was killed in Memphis, Tennessee. His murder sent shock waves

militant: strong in support of something   **brewery** (**broo** ur ee): a factory that makes beer through the nation. For many people, hope seemed to vanish after that violent act. Although many cities around the United States erupted in riots, Father Groppi and others wanted everyone to stay calm, and there were no riots in Milwaukee. Instead, Father Groppi and the Youth Council led a peaceful march of more than 15,000 people to honor Dr. King.

More than 15,000 people marched to honor Dr. King.

Father Groppi and the Youth Council marching for Dr. King

On April 11, President Johnson signed a **federal** fair housing law. Soon after, Milwaukee's mayor proposed that the city pass one too. On April 30, the city council passed a fair housing law that was even stronger than the federal one.

Why did the situation change so quickly? Dr. King's **assassination** pushed politicians across the country to change laws quickly. They hoped that by passing laws against

federal (**fed** ur uhl): having to do with the central government in the United States
assassination (uh **sa** si nay shuhn): the murder of someone well known or important

105

discrimination, black people would see that things were changing for the better and wouldn't riot. These laws were victories against discrimination, but they came only after the tragic murder of Dr. King.

The battle for fair housing laws was won, although it took more than marches in Milwaukee to finally get the law passed. In the process, Father Groppi received national attention, and he became both admired and hated among Milwaukee citizens.

10

Priest and Leader

Even when Father Groppi led protests and marches, he kept performing his job as a priest. He taught about the Bible and civil rights in his sermons. His services often included spirituals like "Swing Low, Sweet Chariot" and "Mary Had a Baby," as well as freedom songs like "We Shall Overcome" and "Ain't Gonna Let Nobody Turn Me Around." He preached about discrimination and the need to stand up against injustice.

Along with all his protest work, Father Groppi still worked hard to be a good priest.

As he led masses, he often used a **call-and-response** pattern in his sermons. He would ask a question and the audience would answer, sometimes echoing what he said. Call-and-response has a long history in African music and language.

One part of a service went like this.

Father Groppi said, "What did **Dick Gregory** mean when he said, 'You take all the people in the world and subtract myself, they're all my brothers and sisters.'"

Someone shouted back, "Everybody in the world is his brother and sister."

Father Groppi said, "What do we mean by black power? Does it mean black people over white people?"

Someone answered, "No, equal. It means opportunity."

Father Groppi said, "What kind of power do we call it?"

Several people shouted out, "Money power, economic power."

---

call-and-response: a pattern of speaking where one person or group says something and another person or group responds with an answer   **Dick Gregory**: an African American comedian and civil rights activist who came to Milwaukee and marched with Father Groppi

Father Groppi said, "What do we mean by political power?"

Someone answered, "We want some black people in office and not just white people."

Father Groppi asked, "What do we mean by educational power?"

Many voices rang out, "We want to get a good education."

Then they sang "We Love Everybody in Our Hearts."

Father Groppi wanted his sermons to connect directly to the lives of the people in the church. "We talk about the sufferings of black people and the injustices of society, the meaning behind black spirituals. The kids listen and they're **reverent**. When we start praying for individuals who have been arrested or have been beaten by the police, they listen, and the Mass suddenly has meaning for them." He knew that people paid more attention to the church's message if they could see how that message applied to their lives and the people they knew.

reverent: showing respect

Sometimes Father Groppi was **soft-spoken**. Other times he was loud and angry. "The Lord ain't gonna help me and he ain't gonna help you unless we get out and help ourselves," he said. And "the greatest Civil Rights worker was Jesus Christ.... You must be **revolutionaries** like he was."

Father Groppi believed in nonviolence, but he had his limits. He once told an audience that he had heard of a 12-year-old girl who was kicked in the stomach by a police officer. "If that ever happens in my presence and I have a baseball bat in my hand, someone is going to get his head bashed in." He was not a violent man, but he could not stand injustice and racism. He was dedicated to protecting those who needed help, and his emotions ran deep.

Father Groppi was once asked why he marched to protest. He gave 3 reasons. First, he said, "It is uniting the Negro ghetto into an interested and effective community."

Also, Father Groppi said, it "forced prejudice to the surface." "Many white citizens have refused to admit that prejudice exists. After the chanting mobs and cursing brick throwers,

soft-spoken: quiet   revolutionary (rev uh **loo** shuhn air ree): someone who wants to change society in a big way

110

WHI IMAGE ID 26543

Father Groppi could not stand injustice and racism.

no one denies the **evidence**."

And third, "It keeps NAACP Youth Council members occupied. If they weren't marching, they'd be throwing firebombs and bricks." Father Groppi knew that the possibility of violence was always present. He wanted people to speak out for their rights, and he also knew that if people were busy with nonviolent protest, they would be less likely to participate in riots.

Father Groppi's work in the civil rights movement in Milwaukee brought him national attention. There were articles

evidence: information and facts that help prove something really happened

about him in newspapers and magazines. During the marches, he was interviewed on the CBS news program *Face the Nation*. He said, "The white man won't do anything for the black man unless he is **disturbed**." He meant that white people wouldn't change on their own; it took civil rights workers and protests to bring change.

Father Groppi was asked to speak to colleges and civil rights organizations. In 1967, the Associated Press, a national news organization, named him "Religious **Newsmaker** of the Year."

While some people loved Father Groppi, others hated him and the work he was doing.

Father Russell Witon was a Catholic priest from a church 30 miles north of Milwaukee. His statements were filled with hatred, and they fed the fires of violence. "We are not going to let those **savages**—those black beasts—take our rights away," he said. "It is the very devil that is behind these people, and we have to pray for their souls." Even though such language was more common in Father Groppi's time than it is

disturbed: upset   **newsmaker**: someone who does something important and gets in the news
savage (**sav** ij): a person who acts in an uncivilized way

today, it was still racism. It shows how deeply prejudice ran in this struggle.

One group of opponents to Father Groppi marched to Archbishop Cousins's home. They carried a casket that read, "God Is White" and "Father Groppi Rest in Hell."

One person who wrote to the newspaper said, "Hey, Groppi, keep your nose out of the South Side. You keep your people in your church and we'll keep ours in our church."

Another one said, "These marches aren't solving anything, only drawing **ridicule** for us Catholics." Other writers threatened Father Groppi with violence.

As a result of being so well known, Father Groppi received many letters from around the country. One letter was simply addressed to "Father so and so, catholic director of black commandos, Milwaukee, Wi." It still got delivered to Father Groppi. He was so famous that the post office knew what the writer meant.

ridicule (rid uh kyool): unkind thoughts and mockery

Father Groppi did not pay much attention to the hate mail. He believed in what he was doing, and he did not let threats or fear stop him.

Other people admired him and sent money and support. Once, a reporter from the *Chicago Sun-Times* interviewed Father Groppi in a fancy Milwaukee home. During the interview, a 10-year-old girl came downstairs and gave Father Groppi $7.50. She had earned it doing housework for several months. "I hope it will help you in your work," she said.

One letter from Louisville, Kentucky, said, "I read with relief that another member of the Catholic clergy has had the courage and the **conviction** to fight with and for the Negro people."

Another from Washington, DC, said, "On reading of you in our local newspaper, my heart went out to you as a real Christian."

conviction: a strong belief or opinion

"I silently march with you," wrote a Canadian nurse, while one white priest wrote, "Thank you for doing what I'm not doing."

A priest from **Tanzania**, Africa, felt that Father Groppi's efforts made it easier to work as a white man in Africa. "I've been hearing about your work on the Voice of America [a radio station] and, as another white priest with a black heart, I want to thank you," he wrote. "Now that a white priest has stood up with our black brothers in America, our presence and our message [in Africa] has been made more acceptable."

One black fourth grader, wrote, "We are Negro and Father Groppi is white, but he help us. We love he. He is helping us get freedom."

Father Groppi had support in the church too. After one riot, Archbishop Cousins defended the actions of all the Catholic priests and nuns who had been involved in civil rights demonstrations. It was clear that he was especially

Tanzania: tan zuh **nee** uh

defending Father Groppi. He said, "They are not the cause of the unrest.... If they were to withdraw completely from the scene, our **minority** and racial problems would still be with us."

Father Groppi was glad when people agreed with him, but if they didn't, he just kept working for civil rights. He was determined. His mind was made up. Even when he was threatened with jail, violence, and death, his vision of a more equal society kept him moving forward.

Archbishop Cousins defended Father Groppi and the marchers.

minority: someone of a small racial or ethnic group that lives among a larger racial or ethnic group

11

After the Marches

Did Father Groppi succeed in his fight for fair housing laws? The protests alone didn't create any new laws. It took Dr. Martin Luther King's death to get politicians to act. But Father Groppi's work brought the problems to everyone's attention in a way that could not be ignored. He was part of the **solution** even if the marches weren't the only reason the Milwaukee fair housing law was passed.

After the fair housing campaign, the people who had worked together went their separate ways. Although fair housing laws were **enacted**, many people felt disappointed that it took the death of Dr. King to get them passed. The marches themselves hadn't been enough.

Soon after, Father Groppi stopped being the advisor to the Youth Council. He was transferred to St. Michael's Church

solution: answer or remedy   **enacted**: officially made a law

in 1970. He continued to work on social justice issues while still performing his duties as a priest with individuals and families.

Over the next few years, he lived in Detroit and Washington, DC, but he always returned to Wisconsin. While in Washington, he hosted a radio talk show for 5 months. "I enjoyed it," he said. "I'd get into a four-hour fight on the air every Saturday night." He liked the challenge of trying to change people's minds.

He also took care of himself by jogging and swimming. He said, "It takes **stamina** and a great deal of strength to work in the streets."

In 1976, Father Groppi married Margaret **Rozga**. Because he got married, Father Groppi wasn't allowed to be a Catholic priest anymore. In the years to come, he and Margaret had 3 children. Father Groppi continued to work for social justice, but he also supported himself by driving a bus and a taxi. He said, "Right now the church will be my bus and people who board it will be my parishioners."

stamina: energy to keep doing something   **Rozga**: roz guh

He spent the rest of his life concerned with other social justice issues in Wisconsin and around the country. He worked for equality for poor people in Wisconsin and Washington, DC. But we remember him most for his leadership in the fair housing marches.

Father Groppi died on November 4, 1985, of brain cancer. His wife, Margaret, later wrote a play about the marches, as well as a book of poems called *200 Nights and One Day*. A journalist named Pete Christensen wrote a **rock opera** about Father Groppi. And in 1988, Milwaukee Mayor John Norquist officially renamed the Sixteenth Street Viaduct the James E. Groppi Unity Bridge in honor of Father Groppi's life and work.

Father Groppi was **passionate** about equal rights. He was a fierce fighter against injustice. Yet despite Father Groppi's commitment and work, his vision of an integrated city still has not been completely accomplished. Although fair housing laws make it easier for people from different backgrounds to live in the same neighborhoods, Milwaukee remains a deeply segregated city.

rock opera: a type of rock and roll album that tries to tell one story through all its songs
passionate (**pash** uh nit): having a great interest in something

Many people did not like his methods, and others disagreed with his beliefs, but Father Groppi worked with thousands of citizens to change Milwaukee. He is the most famous person from Milwaukee's civil rights movement, in which he and many others risked violence, public anger, and **disappointment** to achieve their goals.

In time, we can only hope that what Father Groppi called "the cancer of racism" will disappear. When it does, we will have Father Groppi, and millions of other activists like him, to thank for their work in making Milwaukee, and this country, a more just and equal place to live.

disappointment: being let down or sad when something doesn't work

WHI IMAGE ID 4934

Father Groppi worked to make Milwaukee, and our country, a more just and equal place to live.

Appendix

Father Groppi's Time Line

1930 — James is born in Milwaukee on November 16.

1949 — James graduates from high school.

1950–52 — James attends Mount Calvary Seminary in Fond du Lac, Wisconsin.

1955 — Rosa Parks refuses to give up her seat on the bus in Montgomery, Alabama.

1959 — James graduates from St. Francis Seminary.

1963 — Father Groppi begins working at St. Boniface Church.

Father Groppi attends the March on Washington.

1965 — Civil rights marches occur in Selma, Alabama.

Father Groppi joins the MUSIC protests in Milwaukee and is arrested for the first time.

1966 — Father Groppi and the NAACP Youth Council team up to protest discrimination at the Milwaukee Eagles Club.

1967–68 — Protesters march for 200 days for fair housing in Milwaukee.

1968 — Dr. Martin Luther King Jr. is assassinated on April 4 in Memphis, Tennessee.

1969 — Father Groppi marches with welfare mothers to the capitol in Madison.

1975 — Father Groppi helps in negotiations with Menominee tribes in Gresham, Wisconsin.

1976 — Father Groppi leaves the priesthood and gets married.

1985 — Father Groppi dies of brain cancer on November 4.

Glossary

Pronunciation Key

a cat (kat), pl<u>ai</u>d (plad),
h<u>a</u>lf (haf)

ah f<u>a</u>ther (**fah** THur),
h<u>ear</u>t (hahrt)

air c<u>a</u>rry (**kair** ee), b<u>ear</u> (bair),
wh<u>ere</u> (whair)

aw <u>a</u>ll (awl), l<u>aw</u> (law),
b<u>ough</u>t (bawt)

ay s<u>ay</u> (say), br<u>ea</u>k (brayk),
v<u>ei</u>n (vayn)

e b<u>e</u>t (bet), s<u>ay</u>s (sez),
d<u>ea</u>f (def)

ee b<u>ee</u> (bee), t<u>ea</u>m (teem),
f<u>ear</u> (feer)

i b<u>i</u>t (bit), w<u>o</u>men (**wim** uhn),
b<u>ui</u>ld (bild)

ɪ <u>i</u>ce (ɪs), l<u>ie</u> (lɪ), sk<u>y</u> (skɪ)

o h<u>o</u>t (hot), w<u>a</u>tch (wotch)

oh <u>o</u>pen (**oh** puhn), s<u>ew</u> (soh)

oi b<u>oi</u>l (boil), b<u>oy</u> (boi)

oo p<u>oo</u>l (pool), m<u>o</u>ve (moov),
sh<u>oe</u> (shoo)

or <u>or</u>der (**or** dur), m<u>ore</u> (mor)

ou h<u>ou</u>se (hous), n<u>ow</u> (nou)

u g<u>oo</u>d (gud), sh<u>ou</u>ld (shud)

uh c<u>u</u>p (kuhp), fl<u>oo</u>d (fluhd),
butt<u>o</u>n (**buht** uhn)

ur b<u>ur</u>n (burn), p<u>ear</u>l (purl),
b<u>ir</u>d (burd)

yoo <u>u</u>se (yooz), f<u>ew</u> (fyoo),
v<u>iew</u> (vyoo)

hw <u>wh</u>at (hwuht), <u>wh</u>en (hwen)

TH <u>th</u>at (THat), brea<u>the</u> (breeTH)

zh mea<u>s</u>ure (**mezh** ur),
gara<u>ge</u> (guh **razh**)

accent (**ak** sent): the way you pronounce words and put them together

activist: someone who works to produce political or social change

administration: having to do with the leading and managing of a group

admired: liked and looked up to

alderman: a neighborhood representative

amateur (**am** uh chur): someone who performs without getting paid
    for it

archbishop: the highest-ranking priest in a city or other large area

assassination (uh **sa** si nay shuhn): the murder of someone well known
    or important

associate (uh **soh** see it): someone working with another person

atmosphere (**at** muh sfir): the mood or feeling of a place

Baptist: a large Christian group in the United States

baptize (**bap** tɪz): to sprinkle water on someone's head or dunk him or
    her in water as a sign that the person has become a Christian

beret (buh **ray**): a round, flat hat

bigotry: prejudice

boycott: refusing to buy something or use a service as a protest

brewery (**broo** ur ee): a factory that makes beer

brotherhood: warm and good feelings toward all people, as if they were
    the same as your own brothers or sisters

brutality: violent cruelty

brute: physical rather than intellectual

call-and-response: a pattern of speaking where one person or group says something and another person or group responds with an answer

captivity: the state of being held or kept without freedom

cherry bomb: a small explosive, like a firework

city clerk: a public official who records important information about a city

civil rights movement: the movement during the mid-1950s and 1960s for African Americans to be treated fairly and equally under the law

clergy (**klur** jee): the people trained to lead a religious group, such as priests and rabbis

commando: a member of a military group

committee (kuh **mit** ee): a group of people chosen to meet about a topic and make a decision

confront: deal with something directly

confrontation: a tense or violent meeting

congregation: the group of people who come together for a church service

consumed: had your full attention

conviction: a strong belief or opinion

core: center or middle

council (**cown** suhl): a group of people who run an organization

126

coverage (**kuhv** ur ij): attention

curfew (**kur** fyoo): an order for people not to be outside after a certain time

custom: a habit or common practice of a group of people

dazed (dayzd): stunned and unable to think clearly

decent (**dee** suhnt): acceptable or satisfactory

defend: support or argue for

defying: refusing to obey

demanded: officially and strongly requested

democratic (dem uh **krat** ik): making decision by vote, with everyone having an equal say

demonstration: a public gathering in which people show feelings for or against something

demonstrator: someone taking part in a demonstration

denied: not allowed

desegregated: made to be no longer segregated

determined: strongly wanting to do something

Dick Gregory: an African American comedian and civil rights activist who came to Milwaukee and marched with Father Groppi

dilapidated (duh **lap** uh day tid): run down and falling apart

disappointment: being let down or sad when something doesn't work

discipline (**dis** uh plin): control over the way you act or behave

discrimination: unfair treatment of people, based on differences such as race, age, or place of birth

disperse (**dis** purs): scatter

disrupt: disturb or interrupt

disturbed: upset

docile (**dahs** uhl): calm and easy to lead or teach

eager: interested and excited

economic (ee kah **nahm** ik): having to do with the way a place runs its industry, trade, and finance

eliminate: get rid of

enacted: officially made a law

ensure (en **shur**): make certain that something happens

essay: a piece of writing about a particular subject

eternity: all of time, from the beginning to the end

ethnic: having to do with a group of people sharing the same home country or culture

evidence: information and facts that help prove something really happened

extreme (ek **streem**): very great

federal (**fed** ur uhl): having to do with the central government in the United States

fraternal: having to do with brothers or humanity generally

frustration: a feeling of helplessness and discouragement

gaggle: a group

ghetto (get oh): a usually poor city neighborhood where people of the same race, religion, or ethnic background live, often not by choice

guard: a basketball player who runs the plays on the team

harassed: bothered or annoyed repeatedly

hearse (hurs): a car that carries a coffin during a funeral

heedless: not paying attention to something

heritage (hair uh tij): traditions and culture passed on by ancestors

hostility: strong feelings against someone

housing project: a group of buildings built by the government to give poor people an affordable place to live

human chain: a group of people tightly holding on to each other's arms so that they form a line that can't be easily broken

hypocrite (hip uh krit): a person who claims to believe something but whose actions don't match that belief

immigrant (im uh gruhnt): someone who leaves a country to permanently live in another country

inequality: unfair differences between people

inferior (in **feer** ee ur): not as good

injustice: unfairness or lack of justice

inner-city: having to do with the downtown or central part of a city, usually the poorer and most populated parts of it

integrated: made to include people of all races

juvenile (joo vuh nuhl): childish and immature

legal: allowed by law

legally: in a way that is allowed by law

liberal: in this case, someone who supported civil rights for all

literally: in actual fact and not exaggerated

march: a protest where a lot of people join together publicly to express their opinion about something by walking from one place to another

Marine (muh **reen**): a member of the US Marine Corps, a special branch of the navy

Mass: the main religious service in the Catholic Church

massacre (mass uh ker): a cruel act of killing innocent or defenseless people

migration (mɪ **gray** shuhn): movement from one community to another in the same country

militant: strong in support of something

minority: someone of a small racial or ethnic group that lives among a larger racial or ethnic group

minstrel (min struhl): a performer who sings songs, tells stories and jokes, and recites poetry

mission (mish uhn): a particular task given to a person or group to carry out

National Guard: a volunteer military that is commanded by each state's governor

negotiation (ni goh shee **ay** shun): a discussion of something in order to come to an agreement

newsmaker: someone who does something important and gets in the news

nonviolent civil disobedience: refusing to follow laws and not fighting back when arrested, with the goal of getting the government to change the way things are

ordained: officially made a priest or minister

ordinance: a law issued by a government

outgoing: confident and willing to engage others

overcome: to deal with or get past a problem or challenge

parish: the area and people that a single church is responsible for

parishioner: a member of a parish

passionate (pash uh nit): having a great interest in something

persuade (per **swayd**): convince

petition (puh **ti** shun): a letter signed by many people asking those in power to change a law or rule

picketing: standing outside a place to protest, usually with signs

plantation: a large farm

policy (**pol** uh see): plan of action

political (puh **lit** uh kuhl): having to do with the way a city, state, or nation governs itself

politician (pol uh **tish** uhn): someone who runs for or holds public office, such as a senator

portrayed: shown in a certain way

poverty: the state of being poor

prejudice (**prej** uh dis): treatment of others based on unfair judgment of them

protest: gather and speak out in public to fight for a cause

racism: the belief that one race is better than another

rafter: a beam that supports a roof

rally: a gathering of a large group of people for a specific cause

registered: officially signed up

reluctantly: not wanting to do something

reputation (rep yoo **tay** shun): a person's worth or character as judged by other people

resign: give up a position or job

reverent: showing respect

revolution: the overthrow of a government or leader

revolutionary (rev uh **loo** shuhn air ree): someone who wants to change society in a big way

rickety: poorly made and likely to fall apart

ridicule (**rid** uh kyool): unkind thoughts and mockery

righteousness (**rɪ** chus nis): moral goodness or rightness

riot (**rɪ** uht): a violent and disordered group of people

rock opera: a type of rock and roll album that tries to tell one story through all its songs

rosary (**roh** suh ree): a string of beads that Catholics use to count out prayers

savage (**sav** ij): a person who acts in an uncivilized way

school board: the group of people in charge of a public school district

scourge (skurj): a source of wide-ranging and great problems

segregated: separated for the purpose of keeping groups apart based on the color of their skin

self-defense: the ability to fight back to protect yourself or the things you own

seminary: a school that trains students to become priests, ministers, or rabbis

sibling (**sib** ling): a brother or sister

sit-in: a protest in which people refuse to leave a business that discriminates

slaughtered (**slaw** turd): killed many people

slogan (**sloh** guhn): a phrase or motto

slum landlord: someone who owns a building for rent but doesn't take good care of it

soft-spoken: quiet

solution: answer or remedy

spiritual (spir uh choo uhl): a type of religious folk song created by African Americans in the South

spittoon (spi **toon**): a small bucket that people spit into when they are chewing tobacco

stamina: energy to keep doing something

stereotype: an overly simple idea or opinion of a person, group, or thing

strict: making someone follow all the rules

suburb: an area with homes and stores located outside the main area of a city

superior: someone with a higher rank or position than others

superstitious: believing things that are based on fear or hope, and not on facts

tactic: a plan or method to achieve a goal

targeted: aimed at

tear gas: a gas that causes pain and irritation in the eyes, often used to break up crowds

telegram: a message that is sent by telegraph

tension: a feeling of nervousness, stress, or suspense

threat: a warning that harm will come if something is not done

threatened: told someone they will be hurt if they don't do as they are told

tinder box: a box for holding tinder, which is something flammable that can be used to start a fire

tolerance: the willingness to accept the customs or beliefs of other people

turbulent: wild, confused, or violent

unconstitutional: against the rules described in the US Constitution

unified: brought together as one, not many

viaduct (**vi** uh duhkt): a large bridge that often crosses a valley or city street

volunteer: someone who offers to do something without getting paid for it

white supremacist (suh **prem** uh sist): a person who believes the white race is better than any other

Reading Group Guide and Activities

Discussion Questions

❖ Father Groppi was a dedicated person, and he led many people in striving for civil rights. What are some of the characteristics that made him a good leader?

❖ Because of the work of civil rights activists, many things have changed for black people over the past 60 years. Can you describe some of these changes? How are African Americans treated differently now than they were in the past? Are there still civil rights problems that need to be changed? What would Father Groppi work to change if he were alive today?

❖ Many civil rights workers practiced civil disobedience. Can you define what civil disobedience means? If a law seems unjust, do you think it is okay to break it? When is civil disobedience justified?

❖ Civil rights activists tried hard to use nonviolent tactics, but riots occurred in some cities. Does violence ever improve society? Is it necessary to fight to change the world?

❖ Are there leaders in the country or the world now who work to bring equality and justice for others? Can you name any? What do they do to try to achieve change? Are their tactics similar to those used in the civil rights movement or different?

Activities

- Interview one or more people who are old enough to remember the civil rights movement. Ask them how they learned about it and if they took part in it. What was their opinion about what was going on? Have their views or thoughts on civil rights changed since the civil rights movement? Present the results of your interview to your class.

- Go to a library or use the Internet to research the civil rights movement. Find out what the key events were. Create a chart or time line to show the important events. Add pictures, names, dates, and places.

- What are different ways to practice nonviolent civil disobedience? Make a chart or presentation comparing different tactics. Show how they each break the law without causing harm. Are any of them more effective at bringing about change? Add pictures and historical examples.

- Listen to recordings of freedom songs from the civil rights movement. Learn one of the songs and sing it as part of a presentation on civil rights.

To Learn More about the Civil Rights Movement

Books

Bausum, Ann. *Freedom Riders: John Lewis and Jim Zwerg on the Front Lines of the Civil Rights Movement.* Washington, DC: National Geographic, 2006.

Bullard, Sara. *Free at Last: A History of the Civil Rights Movement and Those Who Died in the Struggle.* Oxford: Oxford University Press, 1994.

Finlayson, Reggie. *"We Shall Overcome": The History of the American Civil Rights Movement.* Minneapolis: Lerner, 2002.

Rappaport, Doreen. *Free at Last: Stories and Songs of Emancipation.* Illustrated by Shane Evans. Somerville, MA: Candlewick, 2004.

———. *Nobody Gonna' Turn Me 'Round: Songs and Stories of the Civil Rights Movement.* Illustrated by Shane Evans. Somerville, MA: Candlewick, 2006.

Stotts, Stuart. *We Shall Overcome: A Song That Changed the World.* New York: Clarion Books, 2009.

Music

Seeger, Pete. "We Shall Overcome," *If I Had a Hammer: Songs of Hope & Struggle.* Smithsonian Folkways SFW40096, 1998.

Sing for Freedom: The Story of the Civil Rights Movement through Its Songs. Smithsonian Folkways SFW40032, 1992.

Acknowledgments

When I was a child, maybe 7 or 8 years old, my father took me to Soldier Field in Chicago for a rally with Martin Luther King Jr. I don't remember much except for seeing Dr. King riding in the backseat of a convertible, waving to a huge cheering crowd. My family was originally from the South, and there was a very real tension between my parents, who had a deep investment in civil rights, and my southern relatives, who had different attitudes. I am grateful to my parents and their friends for their active engagement with social change and their vision of a more equal society. Their perspectives made my writing of this book possible.

The staff of the Wisconsin Historical Society have marched alongside me across the bridge between idea and finished product. Thanks especially to Katherine Pickett, Mike Nemer, and John Nondorf for their help with production.

Bobbie Malone and I went back and forth with many drafts, shaping Father Groppi's story and making difficult concepts accessible. Andrew White took up where Bobbie left off and brought the book into its final form. I am grateful for the help of both. This book would not have been possible without their guidance and knowledge.

I also appreciate Margaret Rozga's time in looking at the final manuscript and her helpful comments.

I have been fortunate to know and work alongside countless Wisconsin citizens who have given time and energy to causes of peace and justice. Some, like Sam Day, Erwin Knoll, and Laurie Ellen Neustadt, have passed on. Others continue to fight, often against difficult odds, bringing issues to the capitol, the legislature, and even the streets. We are fortunate to live in a state where the ideals of democracy remain alive in many hearts.

I would especially like to thank my friends and family, particularly my wife, Heather, who works tirelessly for a better world that our children, Cerisa, Calli, Simon, and Celeste, and all children, will someday make their own mark upon.

Let freedom ring; keep your eyes on the prize.

The following are a few sources that were helpful as I researched this book:

Aukofer, Frank. *City with a Chance*. Milwaukee: Bruce Publishing, 1968.

Jones, Patrick. *Selma of the North: Civil Rights Insurgency in Milwaukee*. Cambridge, MA: Harvard University Press, 2009.

March on Milwaukee website. "Bibliography." http://www4.uwm .edu/libraries/digilib/march/records/bibliography.cfm.

"The Selma of the North: Interview with Patrick D. Jones." By Mitch Teich. *Lake Effect*, February 25, 2009. http://www.wuwm .com/programs/lake_effect/view_le.php?articleid=660.

Index

This index points you to the pages where you can read about persons, places, and ideas. If you do not find the word you are looking for, try to think of another word that means about the same thing.

When you see a page number in **bold** it means there is a picture on that page.